Reck

AKRON SERIES IN POETRY

AKRON SERIES IN POETRY
Mary Biddinger, Editor

Brittany Cavallaro, *Girl-King*
Jennifer Moore, *The Veronica Maneuver*
Philip Metres, *Pictures at an Exhibition: A Petersburg Album*
Emilia Phillips, *Groundspeed*
Leslie Harrison, *The Book of Endings*
Sandra Simonds, *Further Problems with Pleasure*
Matthew Guenette, *Vasectomania*
Aimée Baker, *Doe*
Anne Barngrover, *Brazen Creature*
Emilia Phillips, *Empty Clip*
Emily Rosko, *Weather Inventions*
Caryl Pagel, *Twice Told*
Tyler Mills, *Hawk Parable*
Brittany Cavallaro, *Unhistorical*
Krystal Languell, *Quite Apart*
Oliver de la Paz, *The Boy in the Labyrinth*
Joshua Harmon, *The Soft Path*
Kimberly Quiogue Andrews, *A Brief History of Fruit*
Emily Corwin, *Sensorium*
Annah Browning, *Witch Doctrine*
Sean Shearer, *Red Lemons*
Heather Green, *No Other Rome*
Jennifer Moore, *Easy Does It*
Emilia Phillips, *Embouchure*
Aimee Seu, *Velvet Hounds*
Charles Jensen, *Instructions between Takeoff and Landing*
Heathen, *Outskirts*
Caryl Pagel, *Free Clean Fill Dirt*
Matthew Guenette, *Doom Scroll*
Carrie Oeding, *If I Could Give You a Line*
Jenny Sadre-Orafai, *Dear Outsiders*
Leslie Harrison, *Reck*

Titles published since 2015.
For a complete listing of titles published in the series,
go to www.uakron.edu/uapress/poetry

Reck

Leslie Harrison

The University of Akron Press
Akron, Ohio

ISBN: 978-1-62922-235-6 (cloth)
ISBN: 978-1-62922-234-9 (paper)
ISBN: 978-1-62922-236-3 (ePDF)
ISBN: 978-1-62922-237-0 (ePub)

A catalog record for this title is available from the Library of Congress.

∞ The paper used in this publication meets the minimum requirements of ANSI/NISO z39.48–1992 (Permanence of Paper).

Cover image: View of the Moon, February 26, 1852, John Adams Whipple (OB-8). Courtesy of John G. Wolbach Library, Harvard College Observatory, Cambridge, Mass. Cover design by Amy Freels.

Reck was designed and typeset in Minion 3 by Amy Freels and printed on sixty-pound natural and bound by Baker & Taylor Publisher Services of Ashland, Ohio.

Produced in conjunction with the University of Akron Affordable Learning Initiative. More information is available at www.uakron.edu/affordablelearning/

Contents

Reck (v)—

1. To take notice of, pay attention to

2. To be alarmed, troubled, distressed by

[& the world in which I loved you]

& the world in which I loved you faltered

& grew hot

& the creatures trembled and fell

& the lace of their existence tattered

& the stitching became unmade

& the lace swallowed itself in a last useless blooming

& nothing came to plunder the flowers

& people kept apocalypse boxes

& fled in the season of fire

& the birds dwindled from the chimney

& sent their silence down into the house

& the vixen stalked the vacant brick rectangles

& hunted the clever mice their hungry brothers

& the mirrors emptied of purpose

& we met each other in the cannibal city

& in the steady rain of bodies

& the people kept doomsday clocks

& pointed the hands toward disaster

& the homeless slept in their own corpses

& we planted flowers planted trees

& breathed the longsinging seasons

& wore the same pollen grains as ornaments on the branches

& the indifferent sun burned our shadows into sidewalks

& lit the long wick of the earth

& candled our bodies like eggs

Covalent

& moths steer by the moon but the bees fly not in the night

& keep it over your left shoulder and it will follow you into the wilderness

& the wilderness has one path

& then you turn and follow the moon deeper into tomorrow

& it abandons you there

& inside the walls of a house the bees make honey the bees make noise

& nobody hears the bees whose house was this

& the bees belong to themselves

& they're mortgaged to the flowers

& the house began life as a flower as a thousand

& the house began death as a massacre

& the bees make honey which is to say a future

& the future is not for us not for me the house or the bees

& to whom shall I leave my things who will want the shining glass

& the stacks of rectangles full of language

& these afternoons

& 17 kinds of tea and a dozen pots grimly holding themselves together

& shared electrons form covalent bonds

& the pots contain animal bone and are therefore made strong

& the house contains the bones of trees and is therefore made strong

& the bees perform geometry and music

& hexagons are also strong

& the abandoned house performs geometry and desire

& the flowers and I have our respective beds

& who will grieve the sleep I gave up who will grieve the hive

& the empty house whose walls rang with song

& dripped with sweetness

Parable of the volcano

& I want you to follow me

& into the forest of no more answers no more questions

& we call this the present tense

& once upon a time nerves made you tense

& the past is a different kind of nervous condition

& I can't keep everyone's trauma straight

& this forest is not old growth this forest hides its trauma everywhere

& mown down for ships masts for walls a roof against the future

& for danger but really for fear

& fear is the present conditional

& danger is the past imperfect

& I want you to leave your various shelters

& start over in the present tense

& Mount Saint Helens is highly dangerous

& covered again in trees

& that forest is not old growth

& pearly everlasting did not last but did come back

& the tiny white avalanche lilies bloom in the wake of fire

& in the dust of a shattered mountain

& sword fern lady fern lily of the valley

& the living can only travel so far into devastation

& this is called the dispersal limit

& where it started is the heart the center is that which recovers last

Shipwreck—domestic

It's like in tinkling the whiskey inside the bell of its tumbler
in blending sugar fruit cream and cold we think of ice

as domestic as a tool we use for delight a tool to delight
this tongue awkward at its own party it's like

we look at this glass at what we can make of sand and fire
at what contains and what cannot be kept

we look at what bears our burdens on
between the ice and this polished deck this deck of oak over water

it's like the bright steel laid for dinner thick in its handles its sunward shine
its liquid silver pretty as a pool of poison and starlight

it's like we don't even think of the vessels of our bodies of how much we live
inside a wreck inside this cold impossible falling

Praise song with coyotes and foxes

For the trees of course their secrets their lives

like old spreading deltas a long clock ticking on

their indifference disdain even their stalwart nature

courage of root and rock their raucous brief birds

resident moths praise for later their ice-burdened deaths

their deaths in thunder crack and shatter

how water can do so much with so little

add acid and even these words become invisible

water in the lungs water for the boats water in the boat

of the body thick in its tidal blue tubes

how rain how the rain-laden clouds turn us

luminous as old paintings sad and sadly beautiful

praise too for the future its greedy infants

their time-turned backs strange fashions for the way

they'll mutter and nod over our dry bones our teeth

full of poison metal and meat

praise for the foxes

who are questions vivid as fire vivid as heat who scream

in the night praise too for those darknesses when the tide

of sleep carries everyone else far from here so that

the foxes and I alone keep vigil awake with the stars

praise for of course my beloved stars their faint light

their deaths the news of which will be kept from us

for years for the light years and the dark

for those hours when what you love has already died

but the news is slow to arrive for the unbreakable speed

of light speed of sound for each and every silent minute

silent hour when you continue on as if nothing awful

had not already happened

                                    for the phone call the one

that said she had been gone already a long time

whole hours while for once I slept in the welter wreckage

and joy of facile dreams for those moments

when the coyotes woke me as if they already knew

and were made sad as if they knew the same moment

her house knew the moment it felt the body's sudden vacancy

felt the body falling in quiet thunder the shock wave

immediate and unthinkable the death recorded here in their dirge

as if the echo of this would not go on arriving

for all the remaining years

Ars poetica—bills of mortality (1690)

& the trees gleam wetly under the lustrous clouds

& behind a water-ribboned window a child draws pictures

& the child draws the man as a branch with the moon above

& draws the moon as hollow

& hollow describes everything we ever loved

& boats houses hearts coffins graves ourselves each other

& the trees must feast on the fallen

& turn sunlight into children

& we are 99% tree

& our children are composed and grown in the dark

& the man is therefore only 1% moon

& the worshipful company of parish clerks counts the dead

& 221 infants with their scant handful of days

& the moon perches on the tree's fragile stalk

& one from *planet-struck*

& the moon causes lunacy

& 24 from that

& the man has small hollow Os for eyes

& a falling leaf instead of a smile

& the child draws the radiant sun spiked with yellow fire

& the window slows the rain

& 106 from *suddenly*

& never draws the dark at all

Charm against sorrow

Someone perched bird-like knees drawn to chin feet on a fat branch

back curved like a broken arch someone was huddled on a dead tree

on a tree like old bone over water someone could find nothing at all

to praise in the cage of skin nothing in the cage of afternoon someone

ached and was empty the way the beaten sky might sometimes be just

like a bruise the way storms leave everything behind to heal itself again

to make itself into something other than a case study for the wind and

for the rain the rain falls from a height so great that nothing survives

the distance the distance here cannot even be measured someone was

watching the rain was trying so hard to solve for sorrow someone
thought

she might be sorrow's solitary bird but someone was instead the whole

damned flock thick and coming constantly apart and in the rain her
nascent

her myriad wings grew too heavy to fly her wet feathers became just

another argument she had already or was always just about to lose

Voyager parable

Today I am downhearted meaning sunken meaning mired

Come and be with me in the places just vacated by the predators

First stillness then the rustle of applause

For the incandescent light of survival

For the mighty who hunger but do not dwell

For the timid in their stillness

Even sound waves are a kind of migration

How somewhere out there so deep in the sky we can't find it

Something is singing a song full of static ecstatic with our survival

Somewhere closer by a cicada is crawling out of itself

It will grow wings and it will die

On the record a tree covered in snow

Even trees begin their lives as a journey

First a fall and then a breaking

On the record violence implied by an ancient wall

On the record my childhood lighthouse

Not one shipwreck weapon predator not one war

If the record migrates in only one direction

We are frail craft we are small fry born into mystery

We sleep in our skin waiting to be woken with touch

On the record a baby cries and someone sings

And the crickets go on chirping

And nothing ever dies

Shipwreck—invitation

Come be with me we have tickets for the end

of the world we have a litany of years marked

by fire by others years marked on our bodies

marked in geographies of skin and isotopes come

as the snow arrives accumulates come let us be mice

crawling in through the gaps in a house this house

made for strangers let us curl inside their spun glass

their sunrise walls stealing food from the sloppy birds

carrying it back to our quiet our stolen space heated

by breath which is to say the living body curled into

the living body curled into hidden cavity this secret

between walls between each other come and tell me

the story the one about how you'll find me outside

in the snow pulling answers down from the clouds

pulling breath in past the ice the raptors past the drifts

how you'll find me invisible and twilit tell me you'll

follow the footprints I leave outside your door how

you'll find them find them please before the winds rise

before the wind comes and takes them back

Corona penumbra

We married in the spring we married the shoulder seasons

their discontents their liminal natures we burned our faces

burned our shoulders with the dying sun we divorced before

we had even been born we lived almost at the same time

we became halves that belonged to other wholes we became

holes in the bodies of those who loved us we were holding out

we were holding our hands with our hands we were busy

keeping our distance we kept to the shadow stood the night

watch we stared out too many windows saw the foxes

the hunting cats we rented rooms and called them homes

we went again and again into the weather we came back

unchanged and the same storm finally came for both of us

and all we will ever have is our bones alight with it

the blue arc of power that lightning strike we married other people

we didn't know how could we have known we both wear wings

wear scars etched into our bones we wear feathers

in our skin we cannot fly we stand in this current we burn

Another letter

I wanted a garden a hand to hold while there a hand

joined by a voice saying look at these bluets look at

these hydrangeas their shock of spark on greengrown

fuses I wanted a space made of order made of reckless

disregard made entirely of force faith and taming

let us imagine the garden and what it says it says that

order exists and is available to us that things hold still

that there is an us at all that the walls made ornamental

with brick and black iron fixtures will endure

look I say to this empty this teeming garden busy resisting

its cages look at the birds their chains made of seasons

made of twig and egg look at the mute sky look then

at the ivy that wants that works daily minute by minute

to tear the walls to dust decades of break and breach

look at it again in winter the way it holds on to the cold stone

as if it were necessary as if it were beloved

The things they know

That it takes eight minutes and twenty seconds for sunlight
to arrive

That light slows or speeds depending on the medium

That this is called the refraction index

That if I were on the moon it would take 1.5 seconds for you
to hear the moment I woke and spoke your name

H. G. Wells: *time is only a kind of space*

Refraction is a change in direction

That gap means you are always somewhere in the past

Poe: *space and duration are one*

That gravity is the way space bends around objects the way time
bends around a body

Einstein: *Space tells matter how to move*

Space is a funny thing even though I am

nowhere near the moon and you are

a curse I work back off the paper after it began
as blessing or prayer

Somewhere north of here I whispered your name before
we ever met somewhere north of here

it had just begun

to snow

Selva oscura

& sometimes the dawn is reason enough

& the light slices open the sky peels back the dark

& the trees keep night wet and sticky in their bark

& the night says thank you to the trees with abundant shadow

& the trees are prison bars

& humans are afraid to enter there

& I am not afraid have never been afraid

& therefore I am not human

& the writer posed a question said woods or hell

& Virgil chose hell

& abandon hope the book said leave it outside

& therefore the forest is full of discarded hope

& full of abrogation

& the animals are lawless and the trees grow where they will

& wild tangle of strangeness

& I chose forest instead of hell

& therefore I am not Virgil

& I walk the trails by the light of the stars

& we are nocturnal

& nocturnal means we belong to the night

& not the other way around

& in the dark we are safe from the predators

& time is the most efficient predator of all

& we are safe from time until we are not

& through the branches the cleardark sky

& look at the sky

& the way night gives us a river of stars asleep in time

& asleep in their own burning

Parable of the moon

& the moon is a train is a headlight headstone is unworn dust

& the moon is alchemy is light stolen reflected transformed

& I am rock unlit dark and I am envy

& the moon has no hands

& you do not care about the moon

& you question my attachments the tethers their driven anchors

& anchors can pull you under a tether is distance elided

& you ask me to dance but correct my posture

& the cold coats everything in ice

& I cannot hear your music

& the trees shine as they shatter

& we do not dance

& the sky holds no answers

& the sky holds no answers

Even the blind see blue

& sleep in the doubled down dark

& the brain wakes or quiets by encounters with blue

& the moon's a vacuum around which the blue night trembles

& blue water trembles at the touch of a boat

& the blind cannot see the boat but know the quiver of water

& what is the use of three blind mice

& next the story goes see how they run

& childhood is cruel

& the ocean will not shut up about the moon's tyranny

& she cut off their tails with a carving knife

& adulthood is cruel

& ladybird ladybird fly away home

& your house is on fire your parents are gone

& our house is on fire my parents are gone

& the stars tear through the blue nights untraceable

& blaze their history distance their defiance

& the blind cannot see the stars

& wait in the dark for the knife the sword the morning

Parable of the dead

& I've burned through three fathers

& holes in the blanket of a life

& I burned also through my only mother

& some fabrics are just made that way

& lace is fabric composed of holes gathered together with thread

& holes picked out in white like snow in a thicket

& who or what will keep me warm

& like a lake framed in thickening ice

& a whole forest is lace reversed

& everyone who ever loved me has died

& that is almost true now will be true later

& the word lace is from the Latin meaning ensnare

& also meaning noose

& the ocean makes lace of water and sand

& the city is a concrete blanket laced with glass and danger

& the stars are holes in the lacewinged dark

& we plant the dead like seeds we forget to tend

& grow gardens of holes

& grow lives made mostly of holes

& all the beautiful the delicate empty spaces

Migration

To write means to drown nothing more

I write you letters which means I drown in specific places the shape of an
alphabet the shape of a paper a face

Here let me erase what I've written

No let me erase the previous beloved to whom I wrote

The globe is full of plastic made to look like snow the bowl is full of things
pretending to be fruit incapable of rot

Fruit is the womb of the plant is the mute salt of hope

To write means to drown in memory the birds clotting in a New Mexico
refuge a crane age 38 years a crane age 7 weeks

The way they sound like traffic raucous in the cornfields the way they
fold themselves up like letters mail themselves across the dry distances

Listen to each season's beckon and call to the body's ceaseless restless tides

Listen to the engine its chambers its clicking valves

The heart invented migration migration its only task

This is what I would say to you

I would tell you how the world retreats as the light fades

the birds hush as they find their perches their pews here

in the church of the coming dark safe for once as houses

safe enough for sleep how the dark erases first the far off

then the nearby until your ability to see becomes limitless

the insistent world pushed back the whole thing on pause

this is the gift I wish for you benediction of a withdrawn

region the night's silences the way nothing requires touch

nothing wants it the way the lake cracks open the forest

the way the lake struck rough with moonlight cracks open

your ribcage and yet nothing needs to leave nothing wants

more than this to be here enclosed and opened and how

not that far away the vacant bodies curl in their labeled

their windowed cages how their polished teeth gleam

in the dim light of their fear how it's so quiet that when

the snow starts you can hear each branch etched in whispers

hear each round whole note of bird spoken by the snow

hear this hymn this lullaby shaped like a tree shaped like

the woods like the hissing rippled lake shaped like what

it is evensong vespers shaped exactly like a prayer

Ars poetica—ink

& the words clot in the ink swirl and congeal

& ink was made of damaged trees damaged ground

& I press the letters from my fingers into the ether

& ink is not the absence of light is all the light taken in

& held (prisoner)

& I write the word light with darkness

& the words stall they stick in my throat

& you know what I'm not saying

& the rain keeps falling this angry miracle

& the rain makes a rising tide inside the land

& our houses are short tethered

& the tide pulls the houses under

& every week we send ourselves to intersect in the pathless city

& guns take the people under

& the cicadas drown before they grow wings

& who will whisper to the sakura when the bees die who will sing

& they don't come in pairs the one queen the thousand others

& so Noah failed to save the bees

& I don't come in pairs

& so the bees saved themselves

& their hives were boats in the flood

& daily they performed rescue

& they grew sad at the funerals

& they missed their dead

& they missed their orchards their food their skies

& I know the feeling

& they hummed a dirge

& we considered the ruin of the land

& it became autumn for the bees

& the skies clouded over

& the rains came and came

& the bees fell like leaves like creatures shot from a blind

This is the letter I would write you

I would call it *Zugunruhe* and know that though I cannot
you can pronounce that word perfectly

I would say today rain the hum and splash of white noise the silvery gray
of a sky obscured and suffering

Today the dogs tucked under comforters slumbering how they always
get sleepy and slow in bad weather like ancient tides still rise inside
their sturdy bodies

like their tall-grass circles before sleep to have a memory that long to
remember

Dark chocolate and hot tea the cradle of an oak drawer full of lace full
of delicate made things

What does an oak tree love is it the sun torching the metabolic fires is
it the thin tubes raising water like a sacrament golden cup held to the
light is it the good dirt crumbling at the root is it the rain

How the rain flows around solids creating them in a fluid sliding in
vacancies when I stand in the rain I am

not cleansed nor made wet I am simply a shape an absence

I remember sometimes being a child and yet my body is not the same
body the same shape the bones

How is it that I love you

You could find salt stains the muted smooth beach pebbles taken into my
mouth the ocean like the rain leaving only a slight shine in its absence

the shine and the salt my own spin cycle listen I was a child

the first time now I am that restlessness before migration the way my body

in the rain turns toward where it thinks you might be how the drops gleam at the pine's small needles how I reach and take one shining drop on my tongue how it tastes

of impossible distance even as reflexively I swallow even as distances both collapse and

lengthen into afternoon into white noise is this feeling so slight so fleeting as all that

Listen every love story has a difficult ending every love is a story listen

It might never stop raining

Parable of the maps

& around us the nation was failing

& inside of us the bees kept dying despite everything

& I drew maps of the paths of fireflies

& tried to understand desire

& drew maps of rain

& hung signs for the bees saying take saying eat

& saying please

& saying please don't leave me

& the rain maps looked like oceans full of wrecks

& the oceans looked like maps of my heart

& vistas of blank blue stunned sometimes by storms

& everything large broken and rusting in the depths

& everywhere gravity

& soft surfaces

& the world was dying

& we lived in it exactly the way we had before

& threw babies into the future as if there were one

Kinship parable

& what if this is all we have—the neverlasting wood

& the ocean dying of plastic

& the yearning for those who also yearn—those unbridgeable
   unbreakable spaces

& the imagined silence among the stars

& what if this is all we have—this brief sleep inside the hearts of clocks

& our one broken beloved moon

& the way our skin crumples into bark

& the endless hungers of men

& the way we say endless when we know better

& the cemeteries we can't live inside

& the graves we approach with longing

& dread

& the dead we collect in ringlets

& the way we make our bodies into nurseries

& into furniture—a bed for the baby to howl from

& buy horses for her shelves that she may know thunder

& make for her a set of teeth from bones collected in the meadow

& make for her a set of wings from the crow's old unneeding

& make for her a heart grown inside the heart of a monster

& call her your daughter

Parable of the dictionary

& all night the sky kept faith with us

& shut away from that glory in a box

& unhinged from movement

& pinned by fabric

& these dream-soaked hibernations

& the constellations drifted to the west

& we dreamt each other in our separate beds

& hidden from the stars

& hidden from each other

& this is the definition of longing

& we are victims in our dreams

& startled by gravity

& unvoiced unhoused

& the sky waited patiently for our return to the world

& the winter snowed like all the fallen stars

& the bats woke up stumbled out of their cold caves

& their wings shredded in the wind like joss paper boats

& nothing to eat but stars nothing but snow

& the bats died by the thousands in the terrible nights between us

& bones as fine as pine needles

& this is the definition of despair

& we rose into our respective days

& put away our dreams

& kept our distances

& we fell through our own slow breathing back into dreams

& woke again unspeaking in the cold

& the bats kept dying

& the scientists picked tiny white bones from their soles

& fought to save what they could

& that is the definition of living

Parable of the elephant (1692)

& the first elephant came to America on a ship called America

& nothing but wind pushing her on

& accompanied by guns

& later America struck a whale off Portsmouth

& returned to port

& people pay to see strangeness pay for danger

& she was a two-year-old girl—some migrants are welcome

& the whale's fate is unknown

& that America rotted in the dock stripped of her metals

& became bullets for future wars

& we are a murderous race

& fragile

& another America struck a reef

& maybe the elephant was named Old Bet

& large must equal old gray must equal old

& maybe Old Bet was the second elephant in America

& foreigners are so hard to tell apart

& one America foundered—from the Latin meaning send to the bottom

& one was filled with stones and deliberately sunk

& that is also foundered

& history lost or added an elephant

& one or both were filled with bullets & deliberately sunk

& 77 from *evil*

& another America struck a reef

& 43 from *drowned*

& Mary's keeper struck her

& Mary killed her keeper

& 1288 from *toothache*

& they lynched Mary

& 18 from *executed*

& another America rammed the dock

& 19 from *murder*

& 400 by elephant in the land of elephants

& 100 elephants by citizen

& these are not good numbers

& one America was expended as a target

& one ran aground

& one struck ice one struck another reef

& scatter the bones

& water them with our tears

& watch nothing grow

here in the last America

Parable of the red planet

I am older – tonight, Master –
but the love is the same –
so are the moon and the
crescent –
        —Emily Dickinson

& tonight *Opportunity* died in a cold place

& what does one small engine matter to weather

& the storm overtakes the body

& the batteries wear down

& the distance between the machine and help

& the dust settling out of the wind like snow

& the red nights everywhere in her eyes

& the shawl of red dust she slept inside

& love at just that much distance

& infinite in the end

& the 14 years she spent alone

& amnesia from age related faults

& last words from Perseverance Valley

& Cape Tribulation

& her sister *Spirit* also dead from the cold

& the storm always arriving

& my battery is running low

& it's getting dark

& the earth sings back into the silence

& into the distance of no help arriving

& *I'll Be Seeing You*

A prayer for our mortality

To begin think of wind river sand silk the various strands

currents how falling moving how leaving can be exactly

that benign a cessation of resistance a species of quiet

abnegation think then of a flame on its wick flickering

in the drift of air small fire stubborn and still alight

holding on in the draft that sifts through a summer screen

the leaves too greenly afire on their piers their waxy wicks

the sleeve's small collapse against your arm in the breeze

think of the current of time how it too swirls eddies and then

abates as sticky afternoon slips into sticky dusk itself slipping

into moonrise into full dark think of the lit window

and you inside the moving the breaking heart of this thing

think of the glass doing its best the shell the egg of your dwelling

the way it cradles you how soft the body's flesh how tender

how there are two of you the unformed fetal you asleep

innocent as weather and the you that paces in all that yolk light the light that spills thick and angular through screen and glass

the light that falls across the trimmed the orderly lawn the way

your shadow hushes the crickets afraid there in the sudden dark

the way it releases them as you vanish into song

Wandering heart parable

& wild but also tethered leashed

& leaps out into lakes pale dawns into landscapes of pleasing mien

& into men

& the body says let it go

& says we're tired of the showoff tired of the *sturm und drang*

& stupid useless pump

& still nightly it slips back into the cavity

& a cavity is a hollowed-out place is the empty dark

& cave is to make the hollow go away the way mines collapse

& mine means to take away extract

& the heart is a skate on a string

& mine means to claim to cling grasp and to own

& the little girl pulls the skate along pretending it is obedient

& she slips the string into the hand of a man

& the skate bobs and skitters as if in the wake of a boat

& the man does not notice

& the heart is the least obedient thing on earth

& truant

& truant means beggar but also miserable

& mine means to salt the earth with sudden fire

& the man does not notice the girl does not notice her skate

& the string breaks

& the world becomes composed of skates careening everywhere

& they're bloody clattering comets

& the man wonders what slight thing has changed

& the girl has wept and looked at last away

& the man is unsettled

& stares at his empty hands

& the body wakes with the tail of a comet in its throat

Shipwreck—the ark

The ship has gone down now and there is   nothing left
to be done or undone

this broken swan settles into silt
                                 crumple of rust at rest

we live after every shipwreck live
                              in the wake of a boat

Noah set sail released in time the raven released the dove
    but there was nothing to return for or to

the garden shut the land untamed untouched by salt or hand

no reason to come back no reason
                        except

this winter woodland this glimmerpond at dusk
                        these fine hard blades that carry us

briefly and at speed
                  across glassy silver ice

    nothing to return for but this long glide inside the deepening woods

the woods full of snow full also of silence and invisible creatures
    & the night coming on in murk glitter and spark

nothing to return for except the window glowing somewhere just ahead the window

        sweet as a summer peach

there in the distance

           there in the cold and surrounding dark

We counted the dead

& the people went about in masks

& safe distances

& drank wine over the internet

& sang alone on their balconies

& hoarded yeast while the berries came in from the fields

& rotted in their boxes

& in the year of our lord 1671

& the year of our disaster 2020

& 84 from *colick and wind*

& 43 from *king's evil* which back then was Evil with a capital E

& we whisper the word at the man whose brain is a failure

& who kills by the numbers

& one so far for every day of a year in the city

& I told you to leave me alone

& we nailed the sick into their houses

& left one light on in the theaters

& all the glowing empty stages

& 169 from *rising of the lights*

& the stages of a disaster first blame the other

& then pretend on the beaches

& 78 from *drowned*

& half a million in 78 days

& 62 *killed by several accidents*

& 17 *found dead in the streets*

& quarantine from the Italian for 40

& disasters take no turns

& are not polite

& everyone leaves everyone alone

& they rubbed the sick with bloody birds

& repented with whips in the village greens

& the children play alone in the streets

& corona from crown from the PIE root to bend

& the rain fell upon the earth for 40 days

& 40 nights

& the numbers double and double upon themselves

& 12 from *murdered*

& only 14 from *grief*

& bend but not break

& break from Old English meaning to injure

& to divide solid matter violently into parts

& ashes ashes we buy all the groceries

& I write you letters you will never read

& ashes ashes we need more breathing machines

& the storefronts ache with darkness and stark signs

& closed for the apocalypse

& ashes ashes we all leave work

& 63 from *suddenly* but just 5 from *plague*

& pray for us now in this the hour of our death

& ashes ashes we all fall down

[We lived so long in the fire]

& we lived so long in the fire we got used to the fire

& golden light acetylene blue at the edges

& the withering heat

& we loved the word annealed

& licked and blistered

& all our legends featured snow

& all our dreams were of water

& all our houses were temporary

& all the fish became dragons

& learned to swallow fire

& sheet lightning baked the vacant stars

& every bird a phoenix

& every child a cinder

& every illness a fever

& every lover a river

& all the rivers dried

& the stones filled the beds

& all the questions became matches

& answers lanterns

& all the apertures held oncoming trains

& icebergs were the dream of teeth

& the dream was a balm

& we peeled each other's blackened skin

& put it in our burning mouths

& called it sacrament

Parable of the telephone

& the phone in Japan calls the dead

& what is the country code for missing

& the ocean's an unmarkable grave

& the dead therefore everywhere in the water

& therefore everywhere

& what is the area code for after

& still I call the same number

& hers first then my stepfather's

& they're gone but I kept calling

& what is the exchange for absence

& over and over I tell the sky I'm okay

& not great but okay

& over and over I mow the suburban lawn

& here in this city neither of them ever came to

& here in this unrecognizable house

& the living perform their lives in ten thousand rooms

& we become ghosts to rooms we've left behind

& become for them their dead

& how many more places and houses before I die

& what is the number for sorrow

& operator I want to speak with the wind

& daily call all the dead

& say we miss you we love you the lilacs came back

& I'm drunk on their sweetness

& broken by the way the late snow falls

& clings to their pale their cold lonely faces

Hibernacula parable

& everything increases the wars the numbers the cities

& doors admit people into houses

& gates exclude people from the lands

& we make snow globes those perfect lives under glass

& we imagine skates gliding happily forever across thin ice

& the lights are always on always golden

& beacons steady in their welcome

& the ice never breaks

& nobody goes under

& the fish see etchings in their sky contrails carved by shadows and blades

& there are no guns no roaring silver birds no towers

& even violence causes only weather

& the next storm coats the town with glitter and prism

& even a toy is a lesson in secrets

& the fish are an uncertainty experiment

& deep in the pond we pretend a shipwreck

& the fish are all named Heisenberg

& the people are made unknowable made entirely of secrets

& the absence of touch

& somewhere in the scene a frog has frozen solid

& glucose prevents ice from breaking his heart

& his voice in the spring will be mighty

& spring will never come to the globe

& the one gesture of a tree

& the bare branch the bird endlessly perching

& nobody has to stop skating

& put away the skates and leave the beautiful snow

& go through a doorway

& into another world

& the people glide between the golden lights and the golden fish

& live in sudden storms of shining snow

& they're cradled in distant unreachable hands

& pierced by ice

& saved by sweetness

Tourist parable

& there they are thickets of them tumbleweeds in the sand

& blown across the lands

& wrapped in loud fabric shouting about flowers

& the sad khaki of middle age

& they cannot get a signal

& they wave their devices like fists at the sky

& grow marginally fonder of home

& the sun etches their fluorescent whiteness

& the waves crash in

& we're still breathing shards of god's last breath

& nothing is holy

& this same ocean swallows countless ships unnumbered boats

& the children beg for scoops of frozen sweetness

& we keep sending more ships out onto the water

& the men go sliding in the waves like children on winter hills

& they cannot get a signal

& the ice cream stands are maybe a little holy

& we cannot stop the unforgiving sun

& they press their faces to the glass windows in their hands

& the paper windows in their hands

& the paper plates in their hands

& they're all there at the edge of the land

& facing the blue screen of death

& thinking it is scenery

Collapse

I don't know how to have time make time

buy time don't know how to be on time

as if time were a chair a pony carnival ride

a bike wheeling through the darkening streets

we're careening through space which is also

time and if the stars tell true stories we died

a long time ago which is also to say far from here

we say hello casually this simple acknowledgement

that we're occupying adjacent space occupying

some of the same time we never say goodbye and

one day we'll discover that hello has a past tense

but no future and deep in the night sky a star's

sudden demise will be ancient history and

will astonish lovers and scholars everywhere

Ars poetica—etymology

& we sit beside the toxic waters

& the teeth of creatures litter the beaches

& the bogs the hillsides the ice keep giving back the bodies

& even as ash as isotope the dead never leave us

& the living do

& when the fog lifts off the water

& when the heron lifts out of the water

& scatters glitter in nacreous early light it's an exercise in vanishing

& a magician's trick of misdirect

& exercise means practice

& practice means to follow but only when applied to a course of action

& we all practice the action of turning away

& love is not a course of action but a state of being

& we cannot therefore practice love

& the phrase *love and leave* is attested from 1885

& if the heron comes back is it the same heron

& how could we know

& I said we again though there is no we

& I love that heron its departure into the floating mist

& I try to memorize the cheek, the rough twig legs before it goes

& live and leave share a root

& the root of leave is the causative of stay

& causative means "effective as cause or agent"

& so living causes leaving in the texts

& in the mornings

& really everywhere

Parable of the seasons

& the winter's spunglass sunglass glides into tide and pool

& every empty limb tired of the birds' betrayals

& the leaves ejected from their eden in the air

& the storms that winter all ice and shard all break and shatter

& the house cold and erased in the fields of snow

& me small inside the weather

& the snow retreating

& you were the spring pretending to be mild

& the slaughter of the stars their erasures their ashen tears

& you were the salt-washed roads

& the deer who came to taste that poison danger and wonder

& the white hills inside the white sky inside the white snow

& nesting dolls of distance

& me still small inside the weather

& you were beautiful and graced

& I loved you but you were a man

& therefore of the kingdom animalia

& phylum violence

Parable of the little ghost

& some cultures believe in their ghosts

& the moon is the broken child cast out

& it's this planetary ghost small pale dead thing

& we regard and disregard and blame the moon

& I believe in my ghosts

& they appear not as visions but right here as the living

& some of them I love and some want to kill me

& killing is wrong

& some southern fields grow crops of lead balls

& the water turns to wine and wine turns to blood

& the fields take it back to water and the plants make it into mist

& mist is the ghost of water

& it looks like the ghost of soldiers

& god believes in ghosts it says so right there in the text

& our eyes can never combine red and green some colors are beyond us

& so we have Christmas and the blood-soaked fields

& the people believe in god but not in ghosts

& religion is complicated

& sometimes the text says ghost but means wind means maybe life

& sometimes the text is red

& red means to be spoken by a man

& sometimes the text says ghost but means helper

& the exclamation mark may indicate astonishment or surprise

& perhaps it is rooted in joy

& a dead language

& it looks to me like a lamp casting light

& ghosts were in the text from the start but joy was added after

& in one version there are 275 moments of added joy

& that is a lot of joy

& still it illuminates nothing

Apocalypse looks different than we thought

& the oaks throw their hard their bitter children from the heights

& wait or do not for what might survive

& what might open into growth

& the ocean is full of the lamplit dead

& worn down to isotopes the ones in the bones the ones that identify origin

& therefore catalog longing

& we apply with forms with cards to be merely ourselves

& the ticks fill the meadows with danger

& the ticks fail to fill all the boxes

& we are therefore refused care

& the ocean hides the broken crowded boats

& object lessons shaped like neighbors

& lovers refugees children

& the pollen clings to the empty hives

& settles in the useless lungs

& we watch one mother carry her child through indifferent waters

& push love past death push love past hope

& every bay each inlet is a prayer unanswered

& the dead child weeks later slips under

& our attention drifts toward some other catastrophe

& I keep saying *we* as I assemble papers

& listen to the heart's faltering rhythms

& I keep saying *we* while the virus waits in our faces

& in our untouchable skin

& I keep saying *we* but what I mean is I loved you once

& don't anymore

Whatever is ruined is made strong

& these are the words of god of not your god but my god

& thanks be to god

& they say that after lessons

& after readings from the book which is also lessons

& this is the god who stands after who stands at the end of things

& stands in the rain in the snow

& in the old accumulation of bodies accelerating like a storm

& thanks be to god who made us mortal

& the dead still outnumber the living

& acceleration stops when terminal velocity is reached

& terminal means the end means it's over

& these are the words of the god of the child who watches vultures

& sits chained inside the prison of a classroom

& stays chained to the clanging hours while the playground is picked
clean of bones

& the child who knows broken is not the worst that can happen

& the child who knows the boat needs the weight of its cargo

& without that weight how it goes astray

& too light too fleet for its rudder its keel and sail

& all boats all ships are called *she* and *her*

& so she is filled with stones to steady a transit

& how they steadied the stars under the weight of stories

& how we steer the weighted boats by the weighted stars

& so the sky stays riddled with dead women

& this is called constellation

& the ocean stays riddled with dead women

& this is called shipwreck

& the books of the dead are called the sacred chronology

& the stars are stories men made of women's lives

& the ships are stories the ocean tells for a while

& so the child is never once surprised by how broken we've all become

& how the song on the radio says sorry I don't pray that way

& here in the classroom

& here at the window full of wings and bones the child knows

this is exactly how we pray

A prayer for seven years

Listen I do not want your pity I was a child and I did not speak
did not understand and now the story has no power

I was I still am that one yesterday and the day before and all the ones
that came after listen I loved more than anything my mother

listen this spring to the wings scraping the air raw watch the
    seething shore
I stand on this southern shore

and the spring throws dying birds like vile rain like rain
trying to find its sad its orphaned way home

I stand alone and she has already been gone a long time
and we all know the story how in seven years the body is remade
    inside itself

my hands have been recast as the hands of a stranger
she was my mother and he was not my father and you

are not my lover not my love any longer and all migrations end
but some of us don't ever make it home

so I'll go on moving past the time the hands that forgot her
greet you as a stranger each gesture a flight path to a new shore

where the joss paper boats sail out and I wait for their time to end
all those years ago or here on this shore or later on some other

Shipwreck—what love is

Educated in a series of rectangles marked black

marked red I learned to love in a forest learned

to live I meant to say in a forest love was a thicket

was a city aggressive and lonely full of sharp hard

glass and things pounded flat and as we reached

the outskirts it was all ugly sprawl and strip malls

it was a desert of rectangles and when the train

had wailed on through had cleaved us had made us

cloven and over I learned to live inside the sturdy lives

of trees inside the irregular persistence of a forest

the persistence of its sheltered secret lake the lake

that disappears beneath nothing but itself every winter

Sometimes the winter blows through me

& I tell the truth the way stones do

& indifferent to the torpor of flesh

& its tender bloody meat

& its useless goddamned *feelings*

& sometimes the winter sets up camp like every January night

& I grow exact

& say then that parts of me loved you

& I tried to cut them out with glass with distance

& glass is a super-cooled liquid

& is therefore permanent ice

& glass is indifferent to light

& feelings

& glass makes of distance a picture

& love my love for you is drifted snow

& grown deep but also cold

& snow saves the mice from the sky

& from the raptors the wind the mercury sinking into another night

& snow starves the owls

& obscures the hunger the suffering under something like beauty

& makes leaving even more difficult

& its absence brings the flowers back from their graves

[& say of me this]

& say of me this that I have lived

& lived in the wind its lessons of insistence and yield

& lived in the meadow thrown down by reapers

& shorn by machines

& I have mourned the tiny secret slaughter of the grassborn

& lived inside the grace of horses their swiftness their stonestarred hooves

& lived inside the moon's feral light

& I have been night's creature

& all eyes all ghost

& say of me this I have loved

& part bird caught in a mist net

& part jawbone aching with hunger

& more than half wild

& touch me not unless you mean it

& paint your porch skies blue in my honor

& haint blue made of crushed indigo

& how often we kill beauty to make beauty

& in my time three men

& oh holy oh most murderous men

& say of me this that I loved the sliding wild starlight

& every last guise of water

& the vacant moon the brilliant moon the sad old moon

& worn down to shattered dust

& say of me this I did not want to die

& say I envied all my life the trees their long homes

& their momentary astonishments of birds

& their dreaming canopies aimed at the sky

& their slowspinning years sheltering the meadow

& the way they sang the water into the clouds

& bathed in its return

& each branch like a beseeching

& every branch growing into no better answer

Parable of the spring

& what if spring meant leaves rising into the air

& brushing off the stiff brittle skin of winter

& greening again

& the trees taking back their own disasters

& the ocean floating every miracle wreck back into the air

& what if spring meant battalions of crows rising like helicopters

& circling once and moving into the green distances

& their wings panting like dogs

& before they rose the crows searched the lawns for the bodies of bees

& made of their beaks a cradle

& rock-a-bye baby

& in this way the hive again took flight

& into the treetops

& only the trees knew how to breathe

& the boats tinkled with glass ice and laughter

& sailed gaily along

& when the wind blows

& the sakura petals sang pink into the mornings

& the bees in their keratin nests

& their five aortic arches began again to hum

& the cradle did rock

& nothing but the rain ever fell

& everything healed instead of endlessly starting over

Notes

Selva oscura—Dante's *Inferno* begins thusly: *Nel mezzo del cammin di nostra vita / mi ritrovai per una selva oscura, / ché la diritta via era smarrita.* Loosely translated, "selva oscura" means dark forest or twilit forest.

Even the blind see blue—This poem owes its genesis to a book by Kassia St. Clair called *The Secret Lives of Color.*

Migration—Part of the inspiration for this poem was a visit, with Sasha West, to Bosque del Apache, a National Wildlife Refuge in New Mexico that is a critical resting area for migratory birds, including cranes, which winter over in the refuge.

Voyager parable—the lighthouse in question is the Nubble Light, in York, Maine.

Ars poetica—bills of mortality (1690): This poem and several others use figures from the so-called Bills of Mortality—aggregations of deaths by cause and parish in the city of London during and following the plague years.

The things they know—as far as I know, the quotes are real as attributed.

We counted the dead—This poem draws both from the Bills of Mortality and the counts being kept of infections and deaths due to Covid-19, though by the time you read this, the figures will be wildly, if not catastrophically, out of date.

Apocalypse looks different than we thought—This poem references a female Orca who carried her dead calf for seventeen days and nearly a thousand miles in the Pacific Northwest before letting her go. The Orca's registration number is J35, but she is known as Tahlequah, which, loosely translated from the Cherokee, means two is enough.

Hibernacula parable—Hibernacula are any place a creature seeks out to winter over. Glucose prevents the blood of wood frogs from forming ice shards in freezing temperatures, and this allows them to survive northern winters with part or most of their bodies frozen.

Parable of the telephone—Garden designer Itaru Sasaki installed a one-way telephone in a booth in a garden in Tōhoku province, Japan, in 2010. It was opened to the public in 2011 following the Tōhoku earthquake and tsunami, so that those who wished to could telephone their dead. Sasaki named it the wind phone (風の電話).

Wandering heart parable—takes part of its inspiration from a children's book by Dayal Kaur titled *I Want a Dog*.

Whatever is ruined is made strong—the song in question is "Tainted Love" written by Ed Cobb, first recorded by Gloria Jones in 1964, and made famous by the British pop duo Soft Cell. The quote is from the couplet, "And you think love is to pray / but I'm sorry I don't pray that way."

Acknowledgments

Grateful acknowledgment is made of the editors and journals where these poems first appeared, often in different forms. It is a kind of grace to have thoughtful, intelligent editors in the world doing the hard, good work.

Bennington Review—Kinship parable, Wandering heart parable
Copper Nickel—Parable of the elephant (1692)
Cortland Review—Shipwreck—what love is, Ars poetica—ink
Four Way Review—A prayer for our mortality
Kenyon Review—Collapse, The things they know
Literary Matters—A prayer for seven years, Charm against
     sorrow, Migration
Michigan Quarterly Review—Hibernacula parable
New England Review—Shipwreck—invitation
New Limestone Review—Another letter
On the Seawall—Selva oscura, Shipwreck—the ark
The Paris-American—Corona penumbra
Pleiades—Parable of the maps
Plume—Parable of the little ghost, Voyager parable
Sixth Finch—Ars poetica—etymology, Apocalypse looks different
     than we thought
Tinderbox Poetry Journal—Parable of the dead, Parable of the
     dictionary, This is the letter I would write you
Waxwing—Parable of the telephone, [We lived so long in the fire]
West Branch—Praise song with coyotes and foxes, Shipwreck—
     domestic, This is what I would say to you
Zócolo Public Square—Ars poetica—bills of mortality (1690)

Hibernacula parable was reprinted in *Poetry Daily*.

To Mary Biddinger, Jon Miller, Amy Freels, Thea Ledendecker, Brook Wyers, and everyone at The University of Akron Press: My gratitude continues to know no bounds. Thank you.

The title, *Reck*, is from Jennifer Clarvoe, one of my earliest, most clear-sighted, most trusted readers.

No book happens in a vacuum, and this book especially owes serious debts to the beloved tribe, especially David Bergman, Jennifer Clarvoe, Michael Downs, Amy Freels, Marsha Lucas, Amelia Ostroff, Diana Park, Caroline Plasket, Hallie Richmond, Will Schutt and Tania Biancalani, Jacky Shin, Lisa Sutton, Matt Thorburn, Jeannie Vanasco, Katrina Vandenberg, Sasha West, and Peter Wool. Thanks to the John G. Wolbach Library for the use of the cover image.

And of course, this book is for the ancestors, and for the living poets, too many to list, who are my teachers, whose work I read with endless gratitude and awe.

Photo: Joe Portolano

Leslie Harrison is the author of two previous books, *Displacement* (Mariner, 2009), which won the Bakeless prize in poetry, selected by Eavan Boland, and *The Book of Endings* (Akron, 2017), which was a finalist for the National Book Award. She is a recipient of a National Endowment for the Arts fellowship in poetry and a Mary Sawyers Baker Artist Award. She is a displaced New Englander who lives and works in Baltimore.